BACK TO BASICS

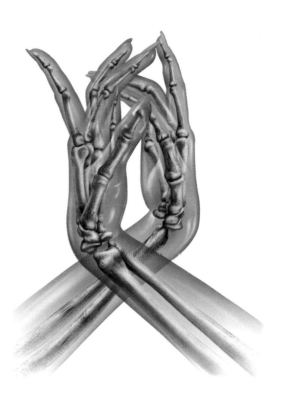

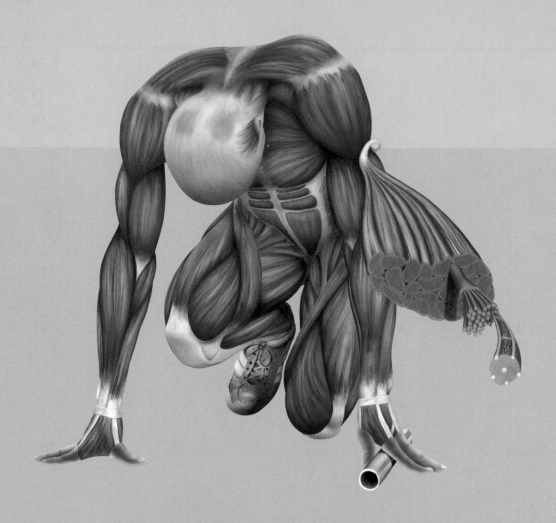

The Back to Basics series was devised and produced by McRae Books Srl, Borgo S. Croce, 8, Florence (Italy)

Publishers: Anne McRae and Marco Nardi
Text: Supplied by Starry Dog Books
Consultant: Sally Morgan
Main Illustrations: Ivan Stalio
Other Illustrations: Lorenzo Cecchi, Paola Holguin, Studio Stalio (Alessandro Cantucci, Fabiano Fabbrucci)
Design: Marco Nardi
Layout: Nick Leggett, Starry Dog Books
Color separations: Fotolito Toscana, Firenze

© 2008 McRae Books Srl, Florence

CIP data available

Printed and bound in Malaysia

BACK TO BASICS

THE HUMAN BODY

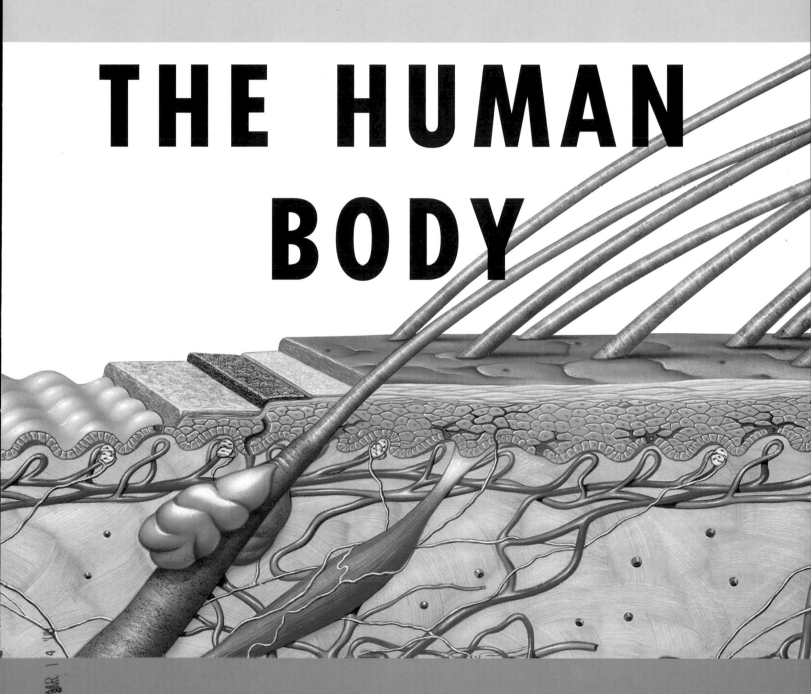

McRae Books

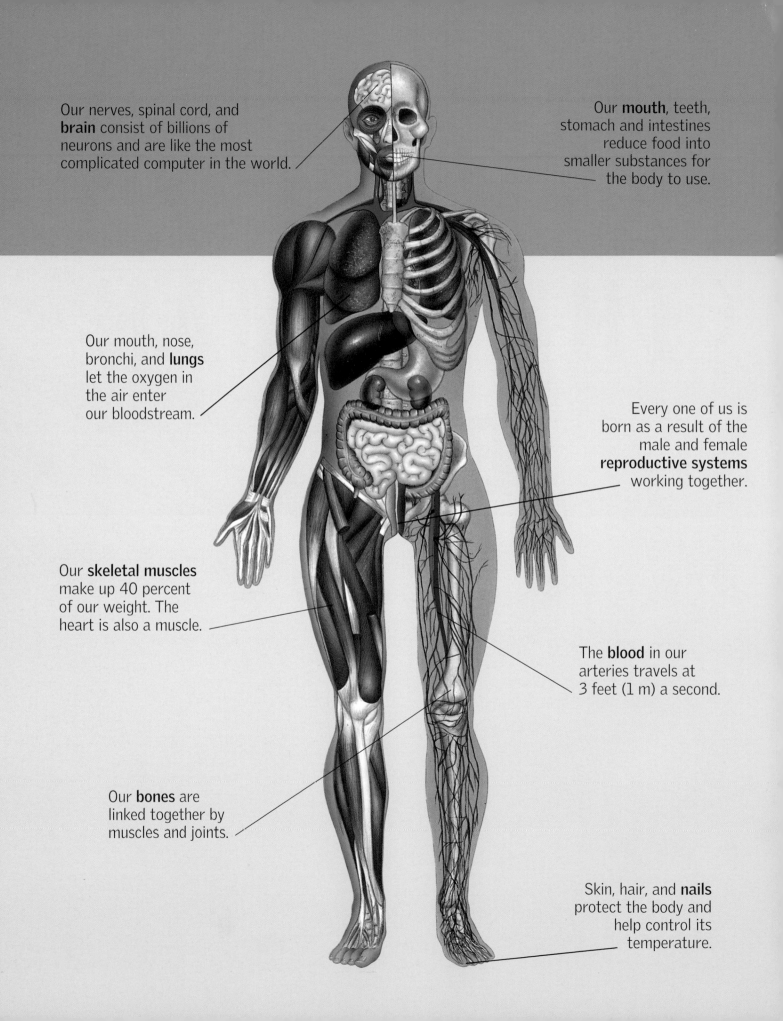

Our nerves, spinal cord, and **brain** consist of billions of neurons and are like the most complicated computer in the world.

Our **mouth**, teeth, stomach and intestines reduce food into smaller substances for the body to use.

Our mouth, nose, bronchi, and **lungs** let the oxygen in the air enter our bloodstream.

Every one of us is born as a result of the male and female **reproductive systems** working together.

Our **skeletal muscles** make up 40 percent of our weight. The heart is also a muscle.

The **blood** in our arteries travels at 3 feet (1 m) a second.

Our **bones** are linked together by muscles and joints.

Skin, hair, and **nails** protect the body and help control its temperature.

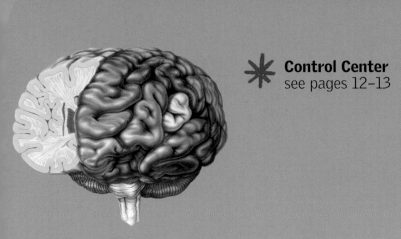

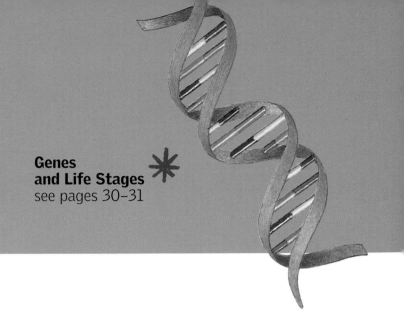

Control Center
see pages 12–13

**Genes
and Life Stages**
see pages 30–31

Contents

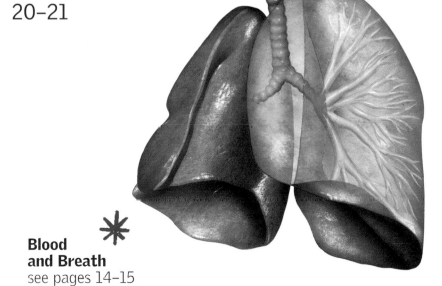

Absorbing Food
see pages 18–19

**Blood
and Breath**
see pages 14–15

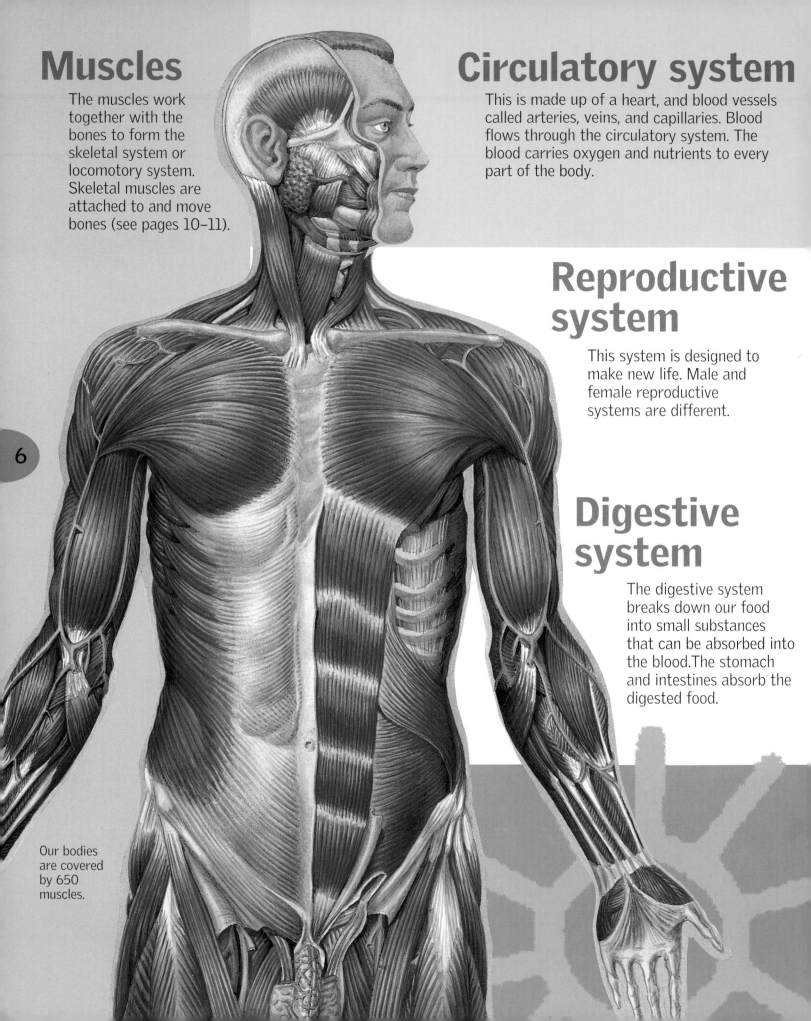

Muscles

The muscles work together with the bones to form the skeletal system or locomotory system. Skeletal muscles are attached to and move bones (see pages 10–11).

Circulatory system

This is made up of a heart, and blood vessels called arteries, veins, and capillaries. Blood flows through the circulatory system. The blood carries oxygen and nutrients to every part of the body.

Reproductive system

This system is designed to make new life. Male and female reproductive systems are different.

Digestive system

The digestive system breaks down our food into small substances that can be absorbed into the blood.The stomach and intestines absorb the digested food.

6

Our bodies are covered by 650 muscles.

Nervous system

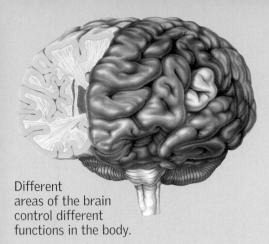

This consists of our brain, spinal cord, and nerves. The nervous system is the control center of our bodies, where actions are planned and carried out.

Different areas of the brain control different functions in the body.

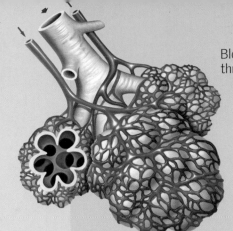

Blood flows through the lungs and picks up oxygen.

Respiratory system

This system allows us to breathe, using our nose, throat, windpipe, and lungs. The oxygen in our lungs passes into our blood.

Let's look at the
Human Body

The human body is like a very complicated machine. It is made up of many different systems, such as the skeletal system (bones and muscles) and the nervous system (brain and nerves). Each system has a special job to do and together the systems do everything we need to stay alive.

Although our bones are hard, our skeletons are very flexible.

Other systems

Other systems in the body include the immune system, which fights against disease, the excretory system, which cleans out waste, and the endocrine system, which makes hormones for growth and other activities.

Skin

Our skin is the largest organ of the body, and is involved in controlling the temperature of our body. Hair, nails, and sweat glands are all part of the skin.

Bones
see page 11

Skeletal system

This system is made up of our bones (an adult has 206) and muscles. Our skull and backbone give us our shape. Our arms and legs enable us to move around.

Inside a cell

A cell is essentially a squidgy case of chemicals. Its nucleus gives the cell instructions for making the chemicals it needs to perform its task. Golgi bodies despatch the chemicals and mitochondria supply the cell with energy.

A close look

Most cells in the body are far too small to be seen by the eye alone. The invention of the microscope in the 17th century allowed people to see cells for the first time. Today, doctors use scanners, imagers, and special cameras to see under the skin.

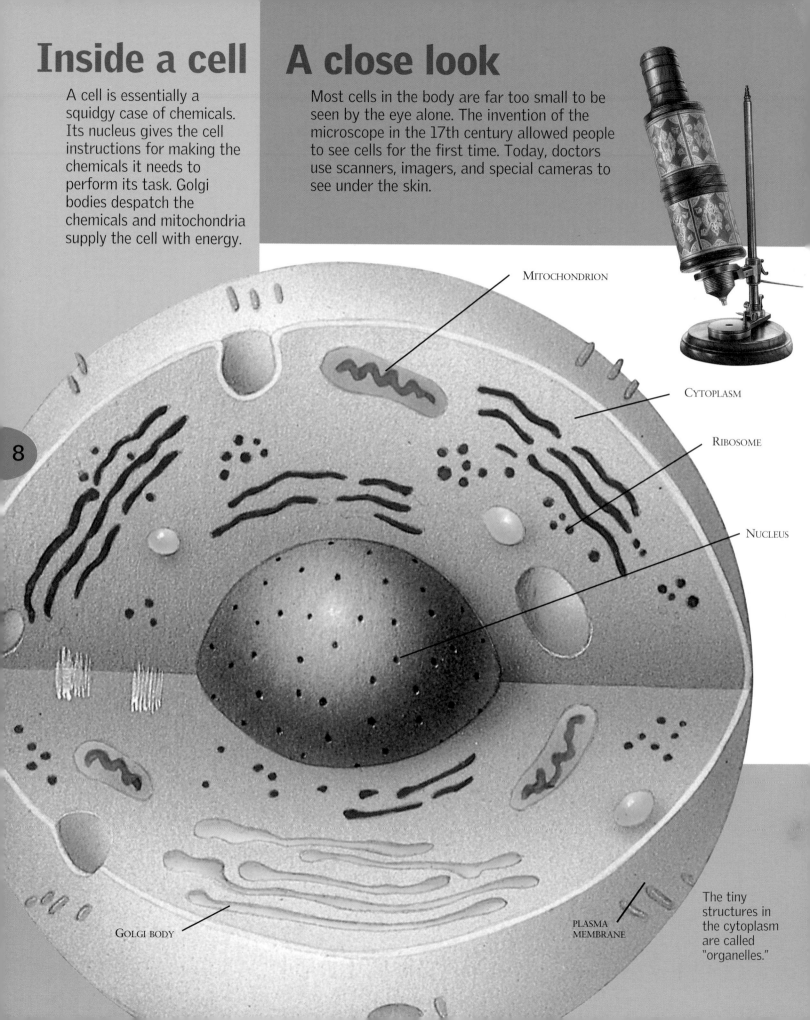

MITOCHONDRION

CYTOPLASM

RIBOSOME

NUCLEUS

GOLGI BODY

PLASMA MEMBRANE

The tiny structures in the cytoplasm are called "organelles."

Cell division

Old cells die and new ones are made all the time inside your body. Most new cells are made through a process called cell division. An original cell splits into two smaller cells. These then grow back to the size of the original cell, and the process begins again.

When a cell splits in two,, each new cell contains a full set of genes (see p.30–31).

Building
Blocks

Cells come in all shapes and sizes, depending on their location and task.

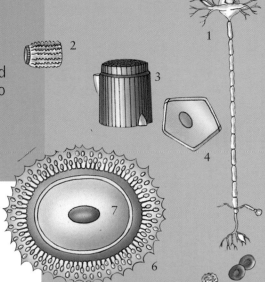

The human body is made up of trillions of tiny cells, too small for the eye to see unaided. There are over 200 kinds in the body, some long and thin, others flat, and some box shaped. Although they may look different, most cells have a similar structure. An outer membrane surrounds a watery jelly, called cytoplasm, which contains a nucleus and various other cell parts. Chemicals made by each cell keep the body running smoothly.

Fat cells lies just under the surface of the skin.

The cells on the top layer of the skin are dead cells.

Tissues

Cells of a similar kind group together to make the body's tissues. Bone cells, for example, make up bone tissue, and cells called neurons form nerve tissue. "Connective" tissue is found between the other types of tissue, and includes fat.

Types of cells

1. Nerve cells
The shape of a nerve cell, with its many branches, enables it to send nerve signals all around the body.
2. Intestine cells
Cells in the lining of the gut live for about 12 hours.
3. Muscle cells
Muscle cells are able to contract or shorten to make muscles work.
4. Skin cells
These cover the body in a protective case that keeps out germs.
5. Blood cells
There are three types of blood cells: red, white, and platelets.
6. Sperm cells
A sperm cell is shaped like a tadpole. It can fertilize a woman's egg cell (ovum).
7. Egg cells
Egg cells are the largest cells in the human body.

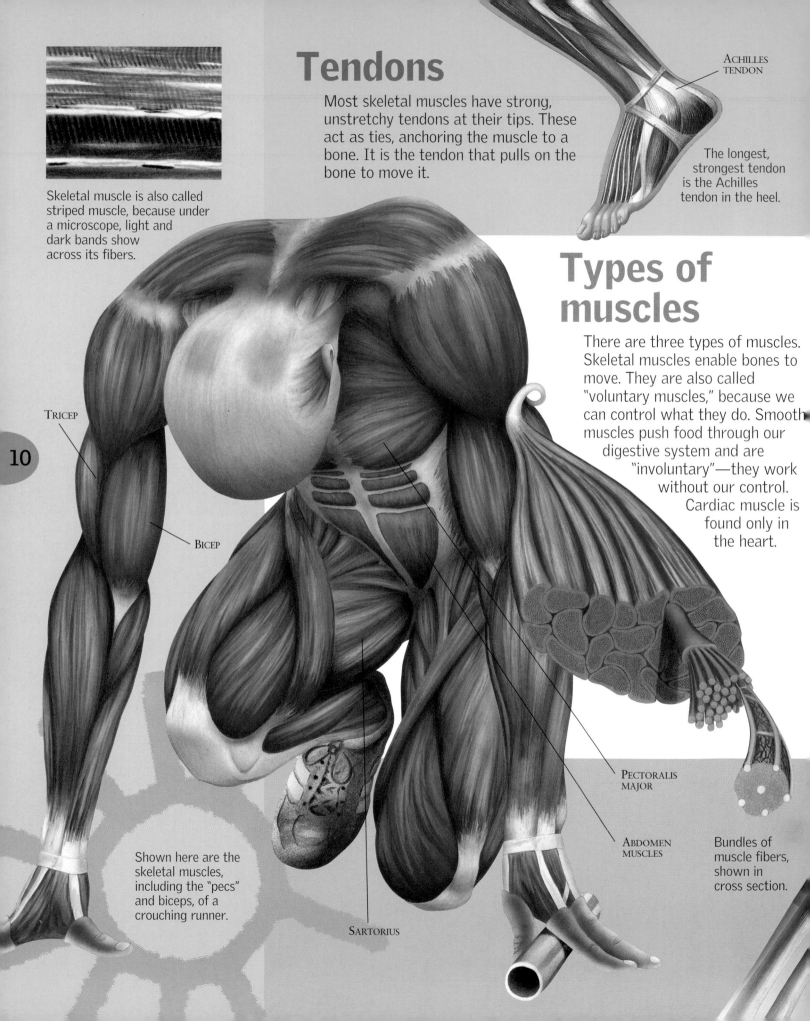

Tendons

Most skeletal muscles have strong, unstretchy tendons at their tips. These act as ties, anchoring the muscle to a bone. It is the tendon that pulls on the bone to move it.

ACHILLES TENDON

The longest, strongest tendon is the Achilles tendon in the heel.

Skeletal muscle is also called striped muscle, because under a microscope, light and dark bands show across its fibers.

Types of muscles

There are three types of muscles. Skeletal muscles enable bones to move. They are also called "voluntary muscles," because we can control what they do. Smooth muscles push food through our digestive system and are "involuntary"—they work without our control. Cardiac muscle is found only in the heart.

TRICEP

BICEP

PECTORALIS MAJOR

ABDOMEN MUSCLES

Bundles of muscle fibers, shown in cross section.

Shown here are the skeletal muscles, including the "pecs" and biceps, of a crouching runner.

SARTORIUS

What are bones like?

Bones are incredibly strong, but also very light. Their tough outer layer (peristeum) is made of calcium and minerals, bound with stretchy collagen. Inside, stress-bearing compact bone surrounds honeycomb-like spongy bone. Down the middle runs soft marrow.

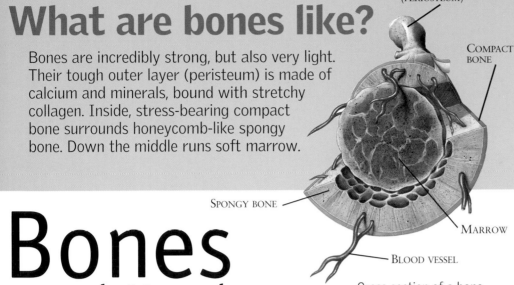

BONE'S OUTER LAYER (PERIOSTEUM)

COMPACT BONE

SPONGY BONE

MARROW

BLOOD VESSEL

Cross section of a bone.

Bones
and Muscles

There are 206 bones in an adult skeleton. Without them, we would look like large jellies. Some bones shield vital organs—the skull, for example, protects our brain. Others help us to move. Bones cannot bend, but the joints where they meet are shaped to allow easy movement. Attached to our bones are 650 different muscles, made from bundles of fibers. Bones, joints, and muscles work together like levers, allowing us a huge range of movements.

Joints

Ball-and-socket joints (shoulders and hips) allow a lot of movement: a round-ended bone swivels in an adjoining cup shape. Hinge joints (elbows) let bones move up and down, while condyloid joints (wrists and knuckles) move up, down, and side to side as well.

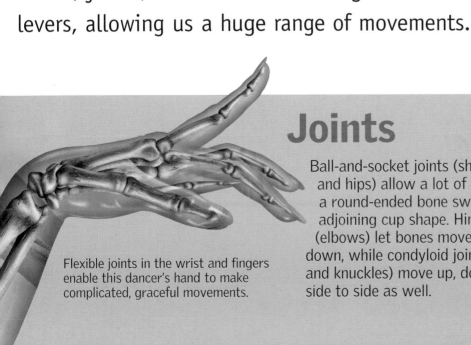

Flexible joints in the wrist and fingers enable this dancer's hand to make complicated, graceful movements.

Bone health

Milk, fish, and dairy products are good for bones. They contain calcium and vitamin D, which help bones to grow strong and not break easily.

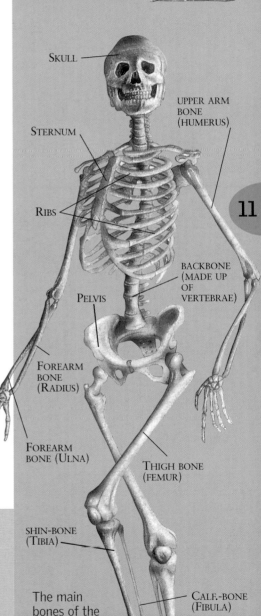

SKULL

STERNUM

RIBS

PELVIS

FOREARM BONE (RADIUS)

FOREARM BONE (ULNA)

UPPER ARM BONE (HUMERUS)

BACKBONE (MADE UP OF VERTEBRAE)

THIGH BONE (FEMUR)

SHIN-BONE (TIBIA)

CALF-BONE (FIBULA)

The main bones of the skeleton. The longest bone, the femur, is about 20 inches (50 cm) in an adult.

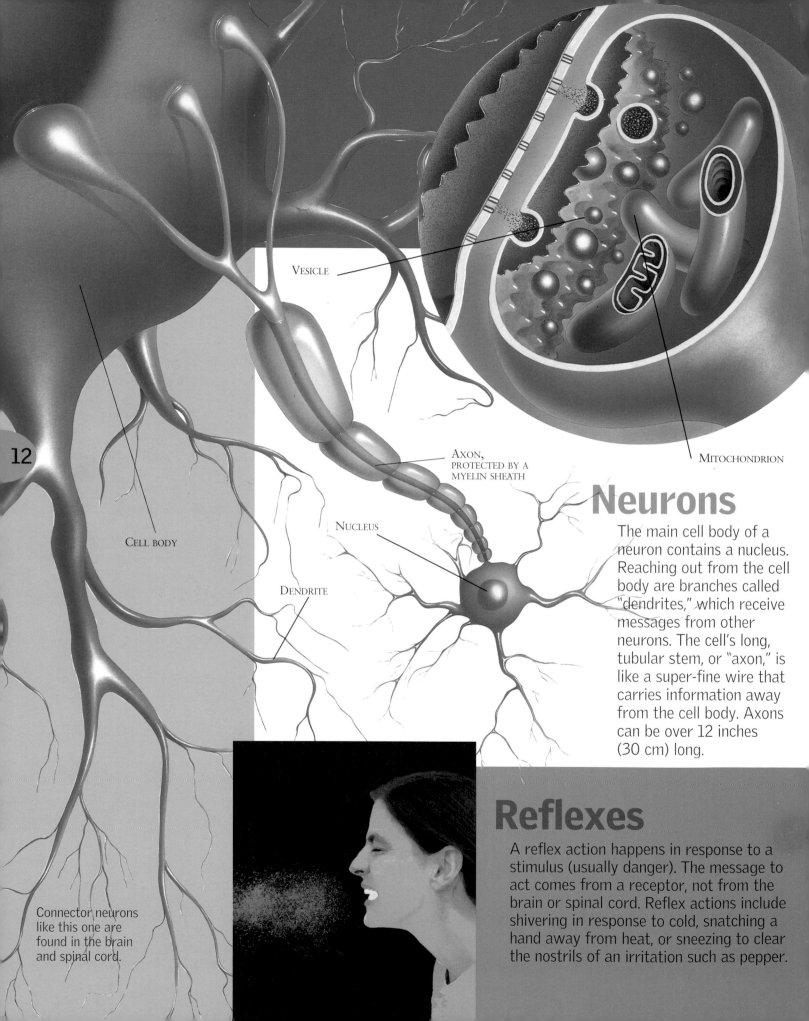

VESICLE

MITOCHONDRION

AXON,
PROTECTED BY A
MYELIN SHEATH

NUCLEUS

CELL BODY

DENDRITE

Neurons

The main cell body of a neuron contains a nucleus. Reaching out from the cell body are branches called "dendrites," which receive messages from other neurons. The cell's long, tubular stem, or "axon," is like a super-fine wire that carries information away from the cell body. Axons can be over 12 inches (30 cm) long.

Connector neurons like this one are found in the brain and spinal cord.

Reflexes

A reflex action happens in response to a stimulus (usually danger). The message to act comes from a receptor, not from the brain or spinal cord. Reflex actions include shivering in response to cold, snatching a hand away from heat, or sneezing to clear the nostrils of an irritation such as pepper.

The brain

There are three distinct parts of the brain. The cerebrum—the largest part—enables us to feel emotions, see, smell, hear, move, remember, speak, and feel hunger and thirst. The cerebellum, at the base of the brain, helps us to balance and coordinate movement. The brain stem controls breathing and coughing, and keeps the heart beating.

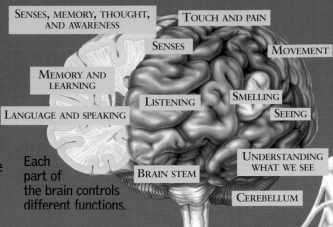

SENSES, MEMORY, THOUGHT, AND AWARENESS

TOUCH AND PAIN

SENSES

MOVEMENT

MEMORY AND LEARNING

LISTENING

SMELLING

LANGUAGE AND SPEAKING

SEEING

UNDERSTANDING WHAT WE SEE

BRAIN STEM

CEREBELLUM

Each part of the brain controls different functions.

Control
Center

The brain controls almost everything we do—it allows us to think, feel, remember, laugh, cry, and move about. It is made from at least 100 million nerve cells, called neurons, which link together in a vast communications network. Bundles of neurons form nerves. Nerves carry messages (tiny electrical pulses) from our sense receptors to the brain, which interprets the information and sends messages back via the nervous system to our organs and muscles.

The nervous system

The brain and spinal cord make up the Central Nervous System. The nerves that extend from the spinal cord to all parts of the body form the Peripheral Nervous System. A third system, the Autonomic Nervous System, controls automatic functions such as heartbeat.

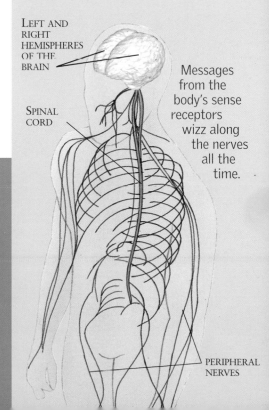

LEFT AND RIGHT HEMISPHERES OF THE BRAIN

SPINAL CORD

Messages from the body's sense receptors wizz along the nerves all the time.

PERIPHERAL NERVES

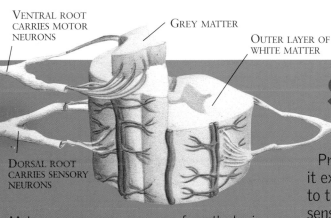

VENTRAL ROOT CARRIES MOTOR NEURONS

GREY MATTER

OUTER LAYER OF WHITE MATTER

DORSAL ROOT CARRIES SENSORY NEURONS

Motor neurons carry messages from the brain to the muscles. Sensory neurons transmit signals from the sense organs to the brain.

Spinal cord

The body's main nerve is the spinal cord. Protected by the backbone, it extends from the brain stem to the lower back. Motor and sensory neurons branch out from the spinal cord through small gaps in the back bones.

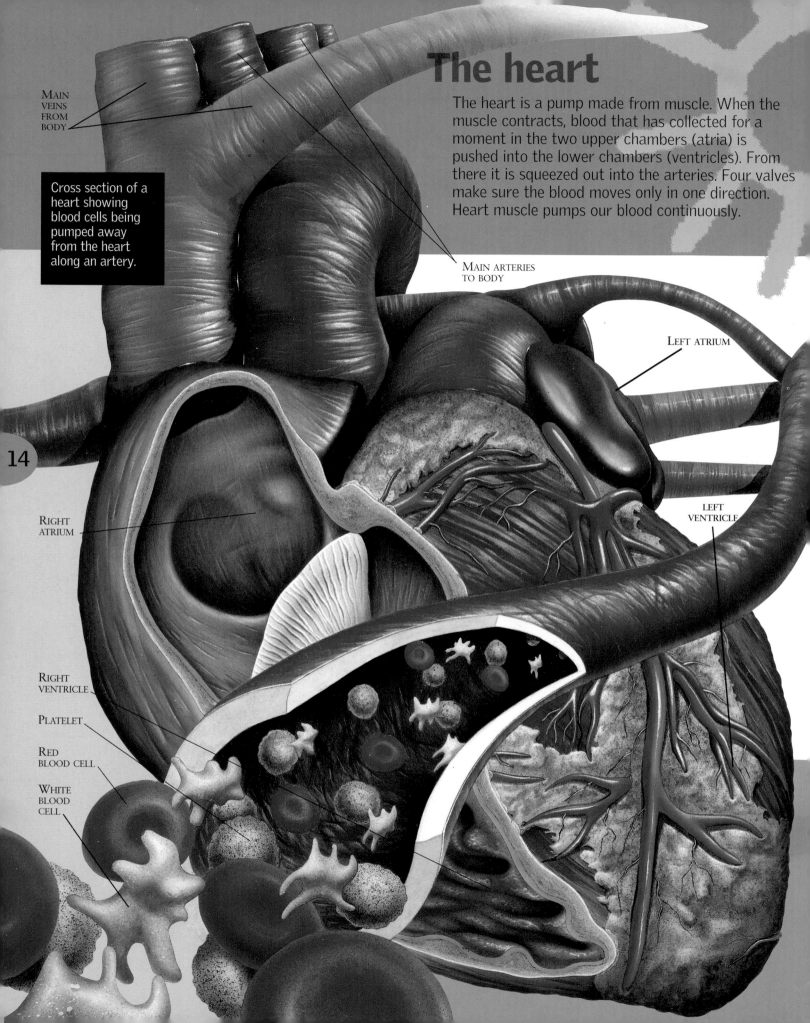

MAIN
VEINS
FROM
BODY

Cross section of a
heart showing
blood cells being
pumped away
from the heart
along an artery.

The heart is a pump made from muscle. When the
muscle contracts, blood that has collected for a
moment in the two upper chambers (atria) is
pushed into the lower chambers (ventricles). From
there it is squeezed out into the arteries. Four valves
make sure the blood moves only in one direction.
Heart muscle pumps our blood continuously.

MAIN ARTERIES
TO BODY

LEFT ATRIUM

14

RIGHT
ATRIUM

LEFT
VENTRICLE

RIGHT
VENTRICLE

PLATELET

RED
BLOOD CELL

WHITE
BLOOD
CELL

Blood cells

Blood contains two main types of cells, red and white, and platelets, which help blood to clot. Red cells contain a protein called haemoglobin, which carries oxygen. Most types of white blood cell are involved in fighting infection.

White blood cells

Red blood cells

Platelet

Circulation

Our heart pumps blood round the body at a rate of about 70 beats a minute. Bright red blood, full of oxygen, travels through arteries. Darker, bluish blood, containing little oxygen, returns through veins.

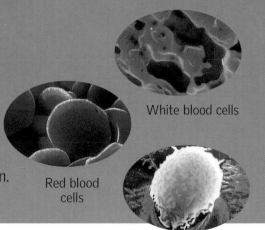

The circulatory system, showing arteries (red) and veins (blue). Tiny capillaries link arteries and veins.

Blood and Breath

Blood is pumped by the heart all round the body. It provides our organs and muscles with the food (nutrients) that they need, and helps to defend us from disease. Blood also transports oxygen to our cells. This oxygen comes into our lungs from the air. Carbon dioxide waste is carried by the blood away from the cells and back to the lungs, and we breathe it out.

(Below) Cross section of our airways. Air makes vocal cords in the larynx vibrate; this lets us make sounds.

EPIGLOTTIS

NOSE

VOICEBOX OR LARYNX

BRONCHIOLES

BRONCHI

LUNGS

Lungs

The air we breathe goes into our lungs—two large, spongy bags in the chest. It travels along two tubes (bronchi) that branch into smaller tubes (bronchioles). At the ends of these are tiny clusters of air sacs called alveoli, each one in a net of blood vessels. Through these alveoli, oxygen is able to enter the bloodstream.

Close-up of alveoli in the lungs.

Airways

The air we breathe in travels down the throat. A flap called the epiglottis stops food from entering the air passage. The air passes through the voicebox (larynx), and goes down the windpipe into the bronchi and lungs.

WINDPIPE

Pituitary gland

The pituitary gland, at the base of the brain, is a master gland that controls other endocrine glands in the body, such as the thyroid, adrenal, and reproductive glands. It also releases growth hormones.

Growth hormones released by the pituitary gland give the message to bone cells to grow during childhood.

Adrenaline makes our heart beat faster as we scream with fear and excitement on a roller-coaster ride.

16

Adrenal glands

Our two adrenal glands produce several different hormones. One helps heal cuts, one helps regulate the balance of water and salt in the body, and a hormone called adrenaline speeds up our heartbeat and breathing when we are scared, excited, or angry.

The glands of the endocrine system, shown here, release their chemicals directly into the bloodstream.

PITUITARY GLAND

THYROID GLAND

THYMUS

ADRENAL GLANDS

PANCREAS

OVARIES (IN FEMALES)

TESTES (IN MALES)

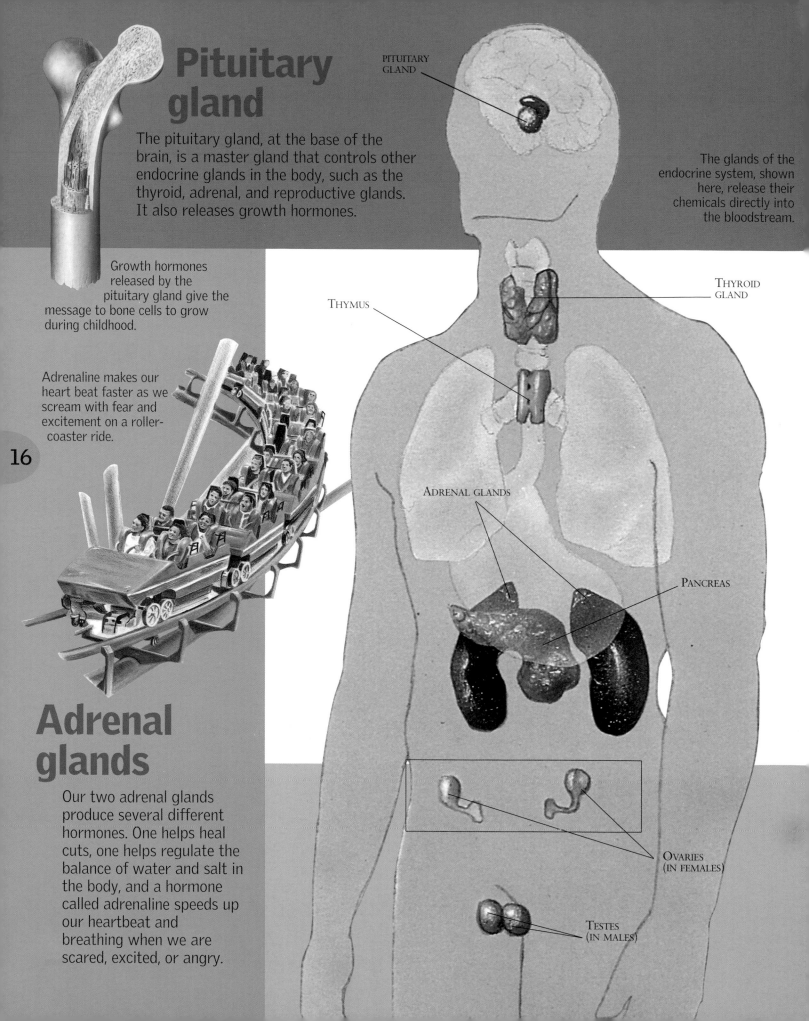

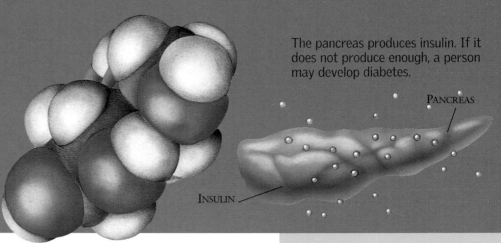

Sugar levels

If we have too much blood glucose (the sugar that the body uses for energy), the pancreas releases a hormone called insulin, which lowers blood glucose levels. If we don't have enough blood glucose, it releases glucagon, which raises blood glucose levels.

The pancreas produces insulin. If it does not produce enough, a person may develop diabetes.

PANCREAS

INSULIN

Chemical
Control

Close-up of a blood glucose molecule.

Certain chemicals in our bodies control some important activities, such as our moods, the speed at which we grow, how fast our heart beats, or when to go to sleep. These chemicals, called hormones, are released into the bloodstream by small organs called endocrine glands. Hormones are chemical messengers. They travel in the bloodstream to the specific body parts that need them, and tell them what to do.

Sex hormones

Sex hormones are involved in sperm and egg production (see pages 24–25). They are produced by glands called the testes in boys and the ovaries in girls. The testes release a hormone called testosterone, which brings on body changes in teenage boys, such as a deeper voice. The ovaries produce the hormones progesterone and oestrogen, which control pregnancy.

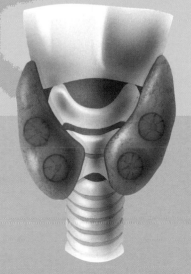

Thyroid and parathyroid glands

Hormones released by the thyroid gland control the rate at which the body "ticks over," or burns energy. If the thyroid works too hard, the body's chemical reactions happen too fast; if it doesn't work hard enough, the chemical reactions are too slow. The four tiny parathyroid glands help control the levels of calcium in the body.

The thyroid gland is shaped like a butterfly; the parathyroid glands are found on the back of the thyroid.

Liver

The body's largest organ, the liver, performs over 500 tasks. One is to check the levels of nutrients in the blood arriving from the villi in the small intestine. When levels are well-balanced, it sends the blood round the body. The liver also stores and distributes sugars, fats, vitamins, and minerals.

Our hard-working teeth are coated in enamel, which is the hardest substance in the body.

Mouth

An adult's mouth has 32 teeth for dealing with food. Four blade-shaped canine teeth and eight incisors are used to bite off food; and eight large pre-molars and 12 molars chew it. Saliva, or spit, helps us swallow food.

Diet

Our diet is the food we eat every day. It should contain a balance of all the elements in food (nutrients) that keep us healthy: carbohydrates (rice, bread); protein (meat, cheese); fats (oily fish) and fiber (cereals), plus plenty of fruit and vegetables.

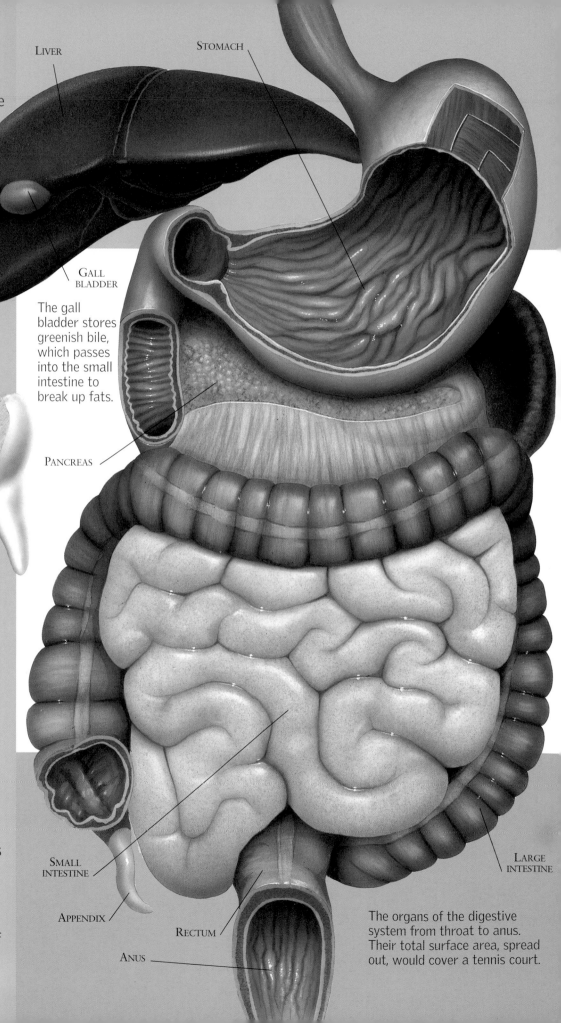

LIVER

STOMACH

GALL
BLADDER

The gall bladder stores greenish bile, which passes into the small intestine to break up fats.

PANCREAS

SMALL
INTESTINE

APPENDIX

RECTUM

ANUS

LARGE
INTESTINE

The organs of the digestive system from throat to anus. Their total surface area, spread out, would cover a tennis court.

Intestines

The small intestine is an incredible 20 feet (6 m) or more long, and lies in a coiled heap under the stomach. Its three sections produce enzymes that finish off the digestion process. Here, nutrients from the food that was eaten are absorbed into the blood. In the large intestine, bacteria process any unused food.

Millions of finger-like villi line the small intestine and absorb nutrients into the blood.

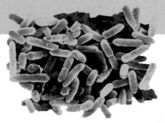

A 1-inch (2.5-cm) layer of bacteria lines the large intestine and deals with food waste.

Absorbing Food

For our bodies to work properly, our cells need energy, which they get from the food we eat. For the food to be useful to our cells, it first has to go through many changes in our digestive system. First, it is swallowed. Then it is squeezed down a tube into the stomach, where it is broken down some more. Finally, it is absorbed into our blood from the liver and small intestine. Waste passes out from the large intestine through the anus.

A long journey

Food goes through four stages on its long journey through the body. We eat it (ingestion). It is broken down by muscle action, acid and chemicals into tiny molecules (digestion). These molecules pass into the bloodstream (absorption), then waste leaves the body (egestion).

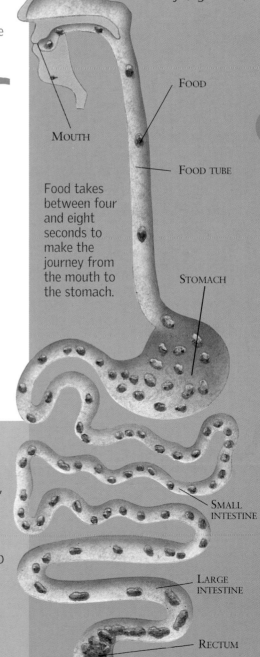

Food takes between four and eight seconds to make the journey from the mouth to the stomach.

MOUTH

FOOD

FOOD TUBE

STOMACH

SMALL INTESTINE

LARGE INTESTINE

RECTUM

19

Stomach

In the stomach, three layers of strong, smooth muscles crush and squeeze our food, and juices with acid reduce it to a thick liquid (chyme). Slimy mucus coats the stomach lining to stop it digesting itself!

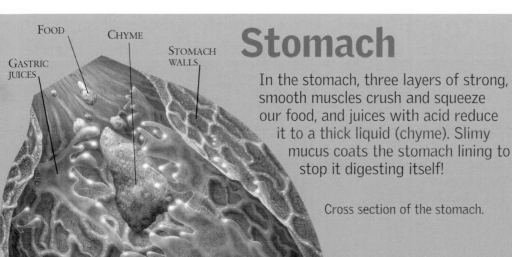

FOOD

CHYME

STOMACH WALLS

GASTRIC JUICES

Cross section of the stomach.

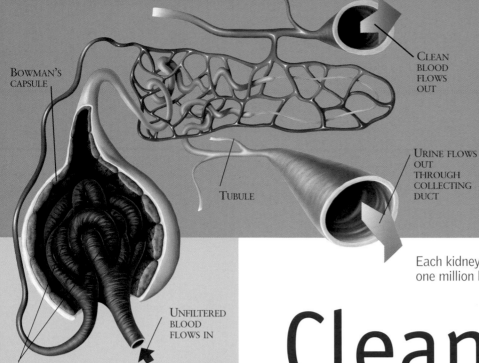

BOWMAN'S CAPSULE

CLEAN BLOOD FLOWS OUT

TUBULE

URINE FLOWS OUT THROUGH COLLECTING DUCT

UNFILTERED BLOOD FLOWS IN

KNOT OF CAPILLARIES

Kidney tubules

Blood passes along tiny capillaries, where water and small substances are squeezed into a kidney tubule. As the water passes along the tubule, the useful substances are removed, and the water and wastes form urine.

Each kidney contains as many as one million kidney tubules.

Cleansing
the Body

As blood flows around your body, it picks up waste materials, such as urea and salts. It is the job of the kidneys to clean the blood by filtering out all of these wastes. The kidneys also control the amount of water in the blood. Excess water and wastes are made into urine, or wee, a watery yellow liquid that leaves your body when you go to the lavatory.

The bladder

The bladder gets larger as it fills with urine. It can hold 600 cm3 (0.6 l or 600 mls) of urine, but a person starts to feel the urge to urinate when the bladder is half full.

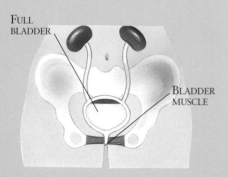

FULL BLADDER

BLADDER MUSCLE

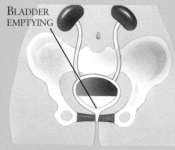

BLADDER EMPTYING

A person produces between one and two liters of urine each day.

Cleaning machine

A dialysis machine is used to clean the blood of people whose kidneys have stopped working. Their blood is cleaned as it flows through the machine.

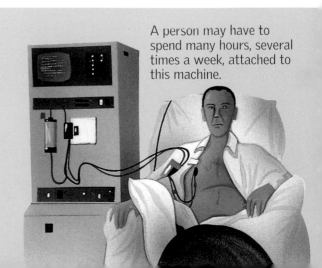

A person may have to spend many hours, several times a week, attached to this machine.

The urinary system

Each kidney is linked to the bladder by a tube called the ureter. The bladder is a muscular bag with a stretchy wall. The bladder is connected to the outside by another tube, the urethra.

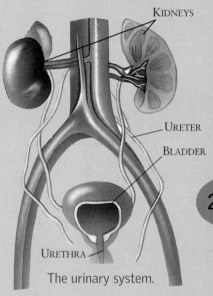

KIDNEYS

URETER

BLADDER

URETHRA

The urinary system.

Water!

Water is essential for life. We get water from food and drinks, but we lose it in urine, and through sweating and breathing.

An adult needs to drink about (6 cups/1.5 liters) of water everyday to stay healthy.

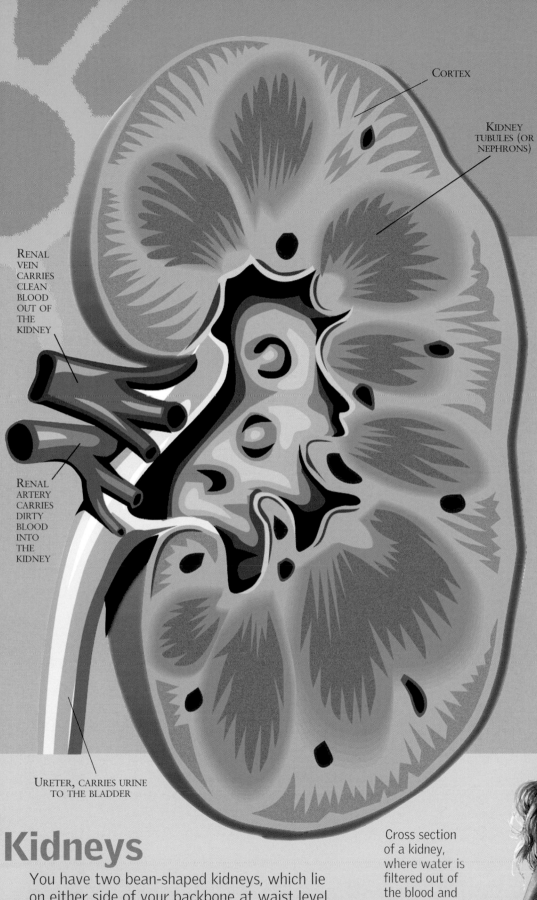

CORTEX

KIDNEY TUBULES (OR NEPHRONS)

RENAL VEIN CARRIES CLEAN BLOOD OUT OF THE KIDNEY

RENAL ARTERY CARRIES DIRTY BLOOD INTO THE KIDNEY

URETER, CARRIES URINE TO THE BLADDER

Kidneys

You have two bean-shaped kidneys, which lie on either side of your backbone at waist level. Each kidney is about the size of a fist. The renal artery brings in blood carrying the wastes. The renal vein carries away the cleaned blood.

Cross section of a kidney, where water is filtered out of the blood and drained off. ("Renal" means relating to the kidney.)

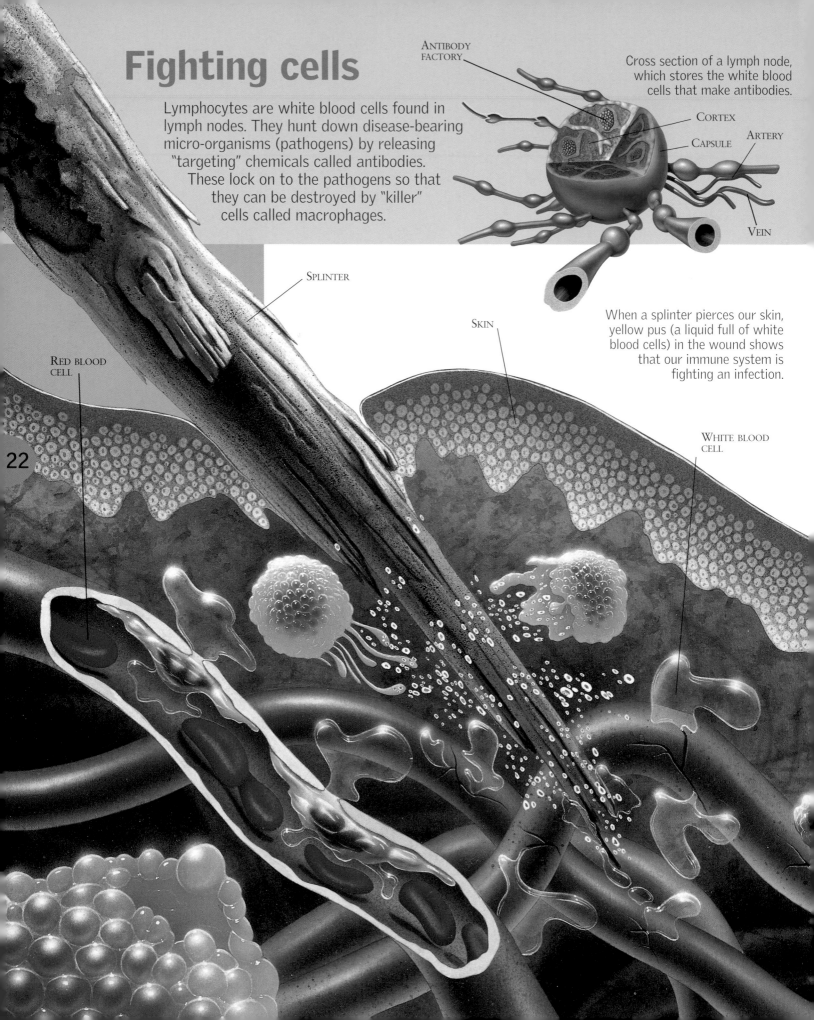

Fighting cells

Lymphocytes are white blood cells found in lymph nodes. They hunt down disease-bearing micro-organisms (pathogens) by releasing "targeting" chemicals called antibodies. These lock on to the pathogens so that they can be destroyed by "killer" cells called macrophages.

ANTIBODY FACTORY

Cross section of a lymph node, which stores the white blood cells that make antibodies.

CORTEX

CAPSULE

ARTERY

VEIN

SPLINTER

SKIN

When a splinter pierces our skin, yellow pus (a liquid full of white blood cells) in the wound shows that our immune system is fighting an infection.

RED BLOOD CELL

WHITE BLOOD CELL

22

Lymphatic system

The lymphatic system extends all over our bodies. Its task is to drain excess fluid from body tissue, clean and filter it in "nodes" and empty it back into blood vessels near the heart. This fluid, called lymph, collects waste from cells and transports white blood cells to attack pathogens.

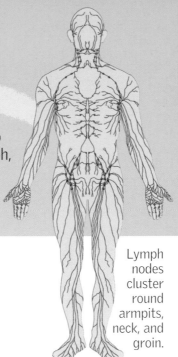

Lymph nodes cluster round armpits, neck, and groin.

Warding off
Enemies

Our body's main enemy is disease, often caused by bacteria or viruses. We fight these in various ways. Antiseptics kill bacteria on the skin, and antibiotics can kill bacteria inside us. Immunization prepares our body's own defenses before diseases attack. Within the body, white blood cells are able to seek out, destroy, and digest invading viruses.

Cancer cells suddenly begin to grow in an uncontrolled way and to overwhelm healthy neighboring cells.

Diseases

Some diseases, like chickenpox, measles, and German measles, are infectious—they can pass from one person to another. Others are not; for instance, smoking is a cause of lung disease. Cell growth that goes wrong causes cancer.

Viruses and bacteria

Viruses are not actually alive, but they can reproduce themselves inside something that lives. All viruses cause diseases: colds, influenza, measles, mumps, AIDS. Bacteria are very simple life forms, found everywhere. Many are useful to us, but others cause diseases: sore throats, boils, food poisoning.

Being immunized

We can be immunized against a disease while we are still healthy by having a weakened dose of the disease injected into our blood. The lymphatic system at once develops white blood cells that contain antibodies to target the disease, should it ever try to invade the body.

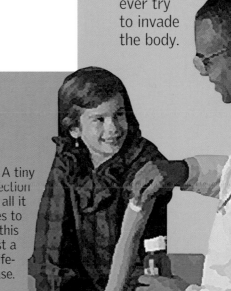

A tiny injection is all it takes to protect this girl against a possibly life-threatening disease.

Stages of pregnancy

A fertilized egg cell rapidly grows and develops, through cell division, into an embryo. By the seventh week of the pregnancy, it has a recognizable head, eyes, and limbs. By the eighth week, it is called a foetus. After about nine months, the baby is born.

A human embryo with a long tail, about 28 days old.

The embryo at about 42 days old.

RIPE EGG (OVUM) BEING RELEASED FROM THE OVARY

UNRIPE EGGS AT DIFFERENT STAGES OF DEVELOPMENT

FOLLICLE, OR SAC-LIKE POUCH

FALLOPIAN TUBE

Cross section of an ovary, showing a ripe egg entering the Fallopian tube, which leads to the womb.

New Life

Reproduction is a process vital to the survival of the human race. It happens when the male and female reproductive systems work together, through sex, to produce a fertilized egg—the first cell of a new baby. The cell now carries the genes (see pages 30–31) of both parents. Inside the womb, the cell rapidly multiplies into millions of cells, which take the form of a human body.

Female reproductive system

When a baby girl is born, she carries inside her thousands of tiny, unripe egg cells. The egg cells are stored in two pouch-like glands called ovaries. From the age of about 10 or 11 years, each month one of her ovaries will release a ripe egg into one of her Fallopian tubes, where it can join up with a sperm cell to make a baby.

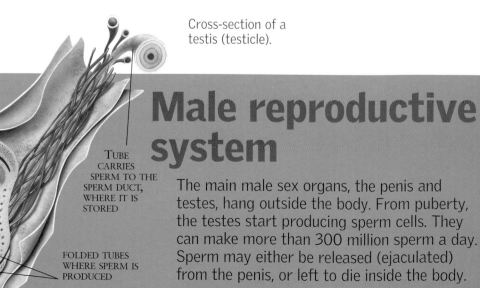

Cross-section of a testis (testicle).

TUBE CARRIES SPERM TO THE SPERM DUCT, WHERE IT IS STORED

FOLDED TUBES WHERE SPERM IS PRODUCED

Male reproductive system

The main male sex organs, the penis and testes, hang outside the body. From puberty, the testes start producing sperm cells. They can make more than 300 million sperm a day. Sperm may either be released (ejaculated) from the penis, or left to die inside the body.

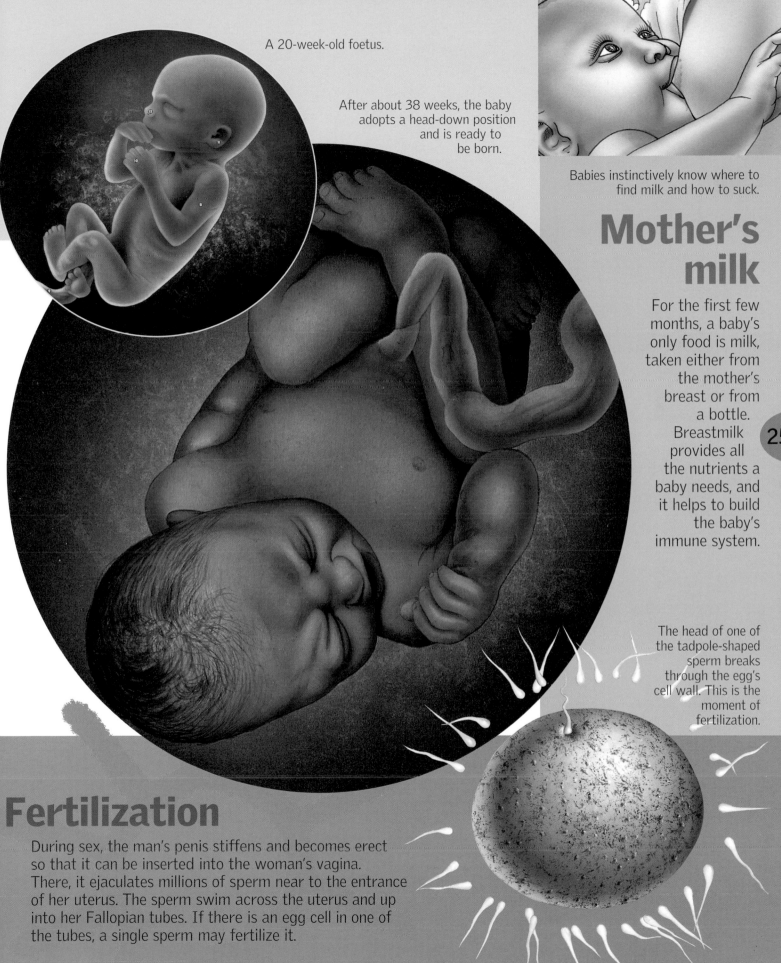

A 20-week-old foetus.

After about 38 weeks, the baby adopts a head-down position and is ready to be born.

Babies instinctively know where to find milk and how to suck.

Mother's milk

For the first few months, a baby's only food is milk, taken either from the mother's breast or from a bottle. Breastmilk provides all the nutrients a baby needs, and it helps to build the baby's immune system.

The head of one of the tadpole-shaped sperm breaks through the egg's cell wall. This is the moment of fertilization.

Fertilization

During sex, the man's penis stiffens and becomes erect so that it can be inserted into the woman's vagina. There, it ejaculates millions of sperm near to the entrance of her uterus. The sperm swim across the uterus and up into her Fallopian tubes. If there is an egg cell in one of the tubes, a single sperm may fertilize it.

Fingerprints

Fingerprints are tiny ridges of skin on the tips of the fingers. The ridges make patterns of arches, swirls, and loops. They are formed on a baby's fingers as it grows in the mother's womb, and don't normally change during a person's lifetime.

No two fingerprints are exactly the same, so they can be used to identify people.

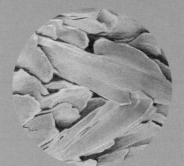

The flat, dead cells of a fingernail tip, seen under a microscope.

Nails

A nail grows from a root embedded in a nail bed made of living cells. As the nail grows, the older cells die and become hard, forming the surface that people clip, file, or paint.

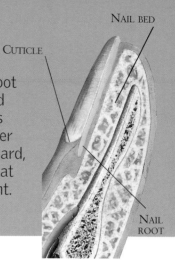

NAIL BED

CUTICLE

NAIL ROOT

Nails protect the ends of our fingers and toes.

The Outer Layer

The skin is a tough but flexible covering that holds the body together and protects the organs from germs, heat, cold, water, and sunlight. The skin has two main layers: the epidermis, or outer covering, and the dermis underneath. Sensors in the dermis make the skin very sensitive and give us our sense of touch. Hair and nails are made from dead cells, so they don't feel anything.

Sweat

If a person's body gets too hot, it produces sweat—a salty liquid made by sweat glands in the dermis layer of the skin. As the sweat reaches the surface via tiny openings called pores, the water evaporates, and this draws heat away from the body.

People with dark skin have a lot of melanin in their skin cells.

People with red hair often have freckles, created when melanin groups together in tiny bunches.

Colors

Hair and skin get their color from cells called melanocytes, which produce a pigment called melanin. If the melanocytes make a lot of melanin, the skin or hair will be dark. If the color-producing cells do not make much melanin, the skin may be pale and the hair blonde.

Old age

As people grow older, their bodies produce less and less melanin. This causes hair to turn white or grey. Some people's cells never produce melanin (a condition called albinism), so they have white skin, white hair, and pale eyes from birth.

Grey hair lacks melanin.

Hair

Fine, short hairs, called "vellus," cover most parts of our bodies. Longer, thicker "terminal" hairs grow on the head. On average, a head has 100,000 strands of hair, which grow about six inches (15 cm) a year.

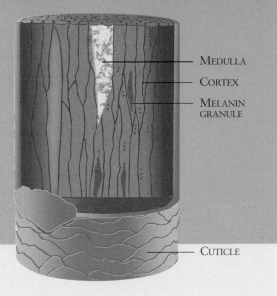

MEDULLA
CORTEX
MELANIN GRANULE
CUTICLE

Cross section of a hair.

Cross section of the skin showing the main structures in the epidermis and dermis layers.

Under the skin

The dermis layer of the skin contains blood vessels, muscle cells, nerves, sweat glands, and hair follicles (roots). The nerves help the body feel cold, heat, pain, and also textures. The sweat glands produce sweat for cooling the body down.

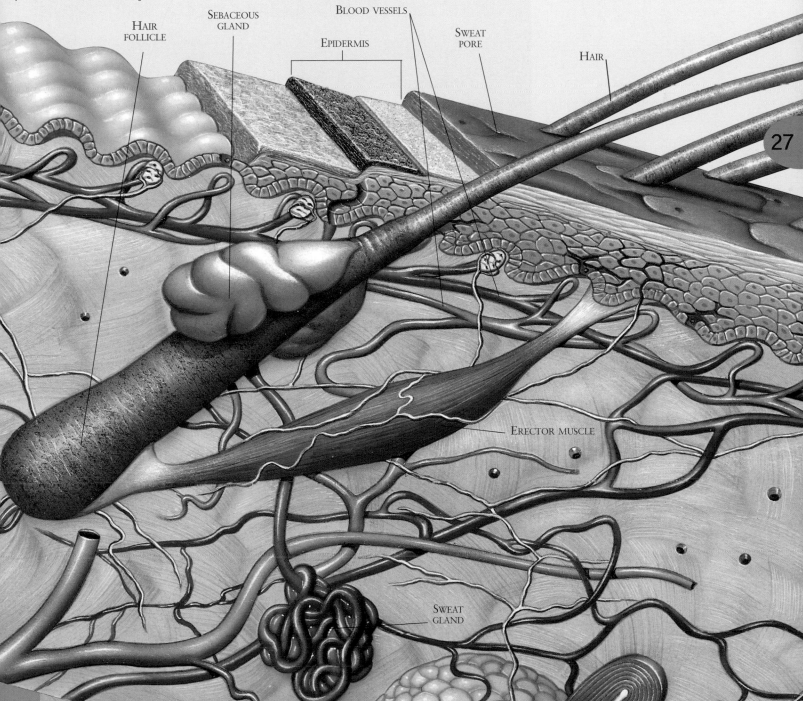

HAIR FOLLICLE
SEBACEOUS GLAND
BLOOD VESSELS
EPIDERMIS
SWEAT PORE
HAIR
ERECTOR MUSCLE
SWEAT GLAND

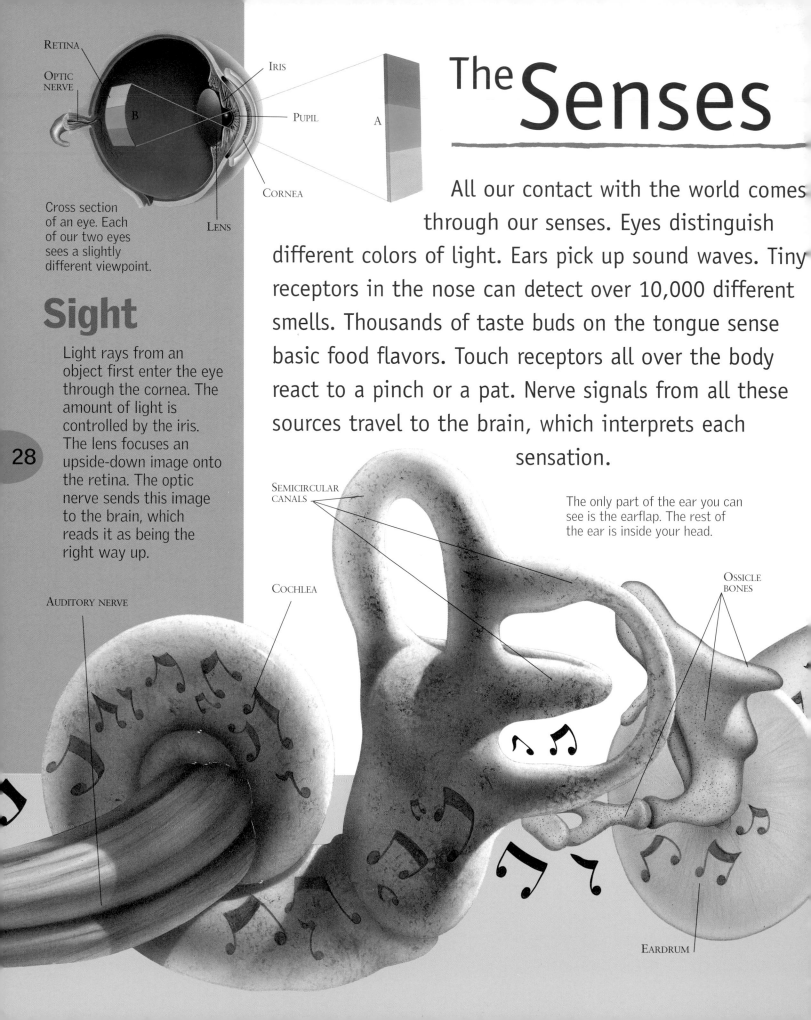

RETINA

OPTIC NERVE

B

IRIS

PUPIL

A

CORNEA

LENS

Cross section of an eye. Each of our two eyes sees a slightly different viewpoint.

Sight

Light rays from an object first enter the eye through the cornea. The amount of light is controlled by the iris. The lens focuses an upside-down image onto the retina. The optic nerve sends this image to the brain, which reads it as being the right way up.

The Senses

All our contact with the world comes through our senses. Eyes distinguish different colors of light. Ears pick up sound waves. Tiny receptors in the nose can detect over 10,000 different smells. Thousands of taste buds on the tongue sense basic food flavors. Touch receptors all over the body react to a pinch or a pat. Nerve signals from all these sources travel to the brain, which interprets each sensation.

SEMICIRCULAR CANALS

The only part of the ear you can see is the earflap. The rest of the ear is inside your head.

OSSICLE BONES

COCHLEA

AUDITORY NERVE

EARDRUM

Touch

Our skin is full of tiny sensors that can detect pain, temperature, and textures. The sensors are attached to nerves, which send signals to the brain about what the skin is feeling.

Blind people can read by touching with their fingertips words "written" in a code of raised dots, a system called Braille.

Cross section of the nose and mouth.

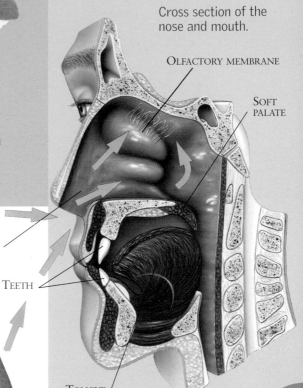

OLFACTORY MEMBRANE

SOFT PALATE

NASAL CAVITY

TEETH

TONGUE

Hearing

Sound waves enter the outer ear through the earflap and pass down the ear canal. In the middle ear, these waves make the eardrum and "ossicle" bones vibrate. This, in turn, causes vibrations in a fluid-filled part of the inner ear called the cochlea. Hair cells in the cochlea's membrane signal down the auditory nerve to the brain, which interprets the signals as sound.

EARFLAP

EAR CANAL

Smell

Smells can please us or warn us of danger—think of food that has "gone off." The olfactory membrane in our nose, no bigger than a stamp, contains five million receptor cells that recognize smells and notify the brain.

Balance

In the ear, three semicircular "canals" contain hair cells. Movement makes fluid in these canals move. This bends the hair cells, which signal the brain to activate muscles that help us balance.

Taste

The tongue can only recognize four tastes: salty, sweet, sour, and bitter. Our more developed sense of smell picks up odors from food in our mouth, helping us to enjoy food more.

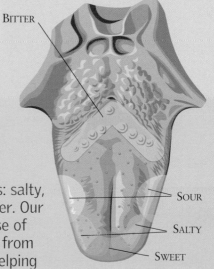

BITTER

SOUR

SALTY

SWEET

Taste map of the tongue.

Chromosomes and DNA

Chromosomes are made of a substance called deoxyribonucleic acid, or DNA for short. Your DNA is what makes you unique—it makes you different from your brother, your mother, and your friends. DNA contains a sugar, a phosphate and four chemicals, called bases.

THE CHEMICAL BASES OF DNA FORM THE RUNGS OF THE LADDER

THE SIDES OF THE LADDER ARE MADE UP OF ALTERNATING SUGAR AND PHOSPHATE

The 23 pairs of human chromosomes.

To see DNA, you would have to use the most powerful of electron microscopes (although even this wouldn't show you the individual bases). This picture shows that each chromosome thread is made up of two strands twisted together, like a spiralling ladder. The ladder-shape is called a double helix.

Genetic Engineering

This branch of science involves changing the DNA of a plant or animal in order to produce desirable characteristics. Plants, for example, can be "engineered" to be hardier or more resistant to disease. Cloning involves making an exact copy of a cell or an individual.

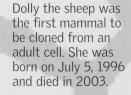

Dolly the sheep was the first mammal to be cloned from an adult cell. She was born on July 5, 1996 and died in 2003.

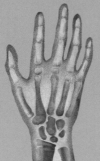
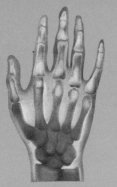
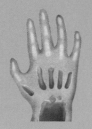

The hand of a one-year-old, with wrist bones not yet developed.

The hand of a three-year-old.

The hand of a 13-year-old.

The hand of a 20-year-old, with bones fully grown.

Changes

Between birth and old age, the body goes through many changes. Throughout childhood, until our early twenties, we get taller as our bones grow longer. In old age our bones weaken, causing some people to stoop and appear shorter.

Genes
and Life Stages

Every human life starts when a sperm cell, with 23 chromosomes in its nucleus, joins with (fertilizes) an egg cell with its own 23 chromosomes, creating a cell with 23 pairs of chromosomes. Chromosomes are made of microscopic threads of a chemical called DNA. A gene is a section of the DNA thread (each chromosome has many genes). Genes provide the chemical codes of instructions that control what your cells do, and how you look.

Twins

There are two kinds of twins. Identical twins happen when a fertilized egg splits into two, forming two babies with the same genes. Fraternal twins are formed when two different eggs are fertilized and implant in the mother's womb at the same time. The genes of fraternal twins are not the same.

Identical twins are always the same sex, because they came from one egg that split into two.

Growing Up

Girls reach puberty at about 10 or 11 years old; boys at 11 or 12. Puberty lasts for several years.

In the preteen years (called puberty), boys and girls start producing sex hormones and their bodies become more like those of adults. Boys may grow hair on their faces and develop deeper voices. Girls grow breasts and broader hips. In puberty, boys and girls often have crushes on adults, and worry more about their appearance than they did as children.

Index